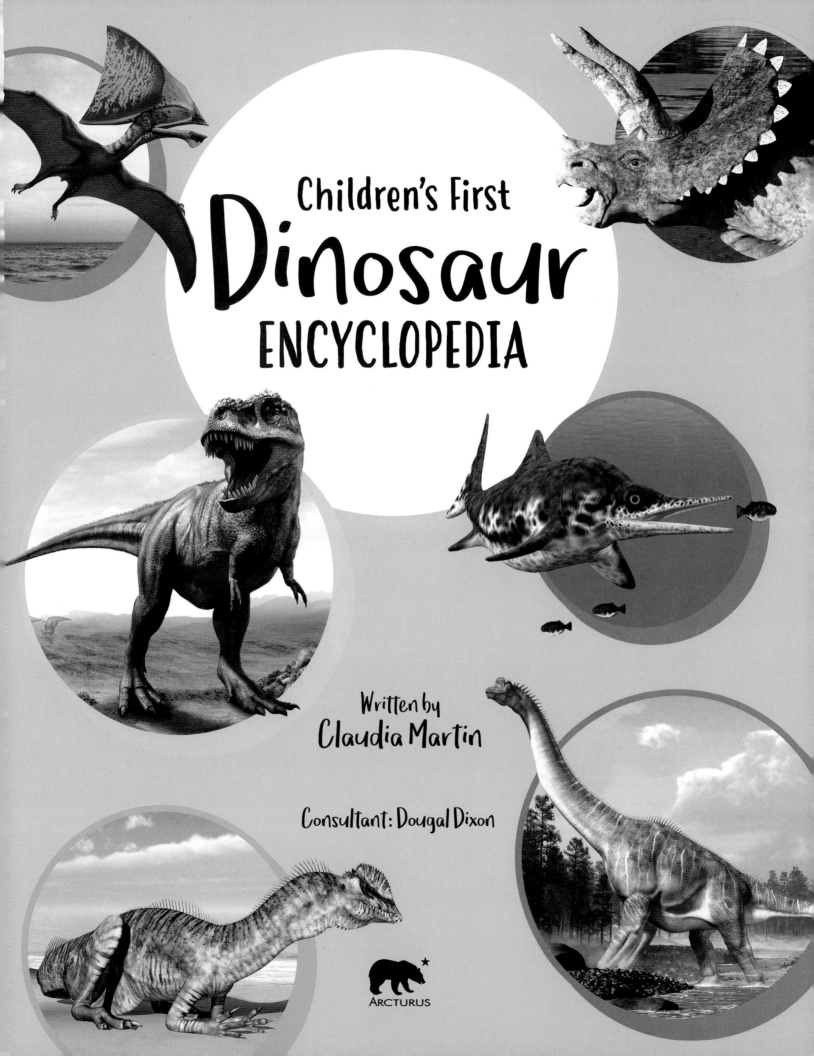

Children's First
Dinosaur
ENCYCLOPEDIA

Written by
Claudia Martin

Consultant: Dougal Dixon

ARCTURUS

Picture Credits:
Key: b = bottom, t = top, c = center, l = left, r = right

Alamy Stock Photo: 1tl, 10–11, 74–75 (Sergey Krasovskiy/Stocktrek Images), 8–9 (Sylvia Buchholz/Reuters), 46–47 (Elena Duvernay/Stocktrek Images), 72–73 (Arthur Dorety/Stocktrek Images), 74b (Sergey Krasovskiy/Stocktrek Images), 81br (Universal Images Group North America LLC/DeAgostini); **Mat Edwards:** 69c; **Science Photo Library:** 8b (Gary Hincks), 13tr (John Sibbick), 20–21, 44–45, 50–51, 70b, 78–79 (James Kuether), 24–25, 38–39 (Mark Garlick), 29tl (Carlton Publishing Group), 35b (Millard H. Sharp/Science Source), 48–49, 80–81, 88br (Jaime Chirinos), 50b, 56c (Natural History Museum, London), 60–61, 88–89 (Walter Myers), 62b (Julius T Csotonyi), 68–69 (Masato Hattori), 75cr (Mark P. Witton), 76bl (Roger Harris); **Shutterstock:** 1cl, 4–5, 5bl, 13bc, 34–35, 40–41c, 42–43, 52–53, 54–55, 66–67, 68br, 71cr, 73bl, 76–77, 86–87 (Warpaint), 1br, 4c, 6–7, 12–13, 14–15, 16–17, 22–23, 22c, 26–27, 27cr, 28–29, 30–31, 32–33, 34c, 36–37, 48c, 49br, 57tl, 58–59, 59c, 62–63, 70–71, 82–83, 83t, 84–85 (Daniel Eskridge), 1cr, 1bl, 5tr, 30bl, 33cr, 66br, 79c, 84cl, 86bl, 92–93, 92c, 95b (Michael Rosskothen), 6b (miha de), 7tl, 16cl, 17b, 18–19, 19cr, 21cr, 23t, 41tr, 46br, 53cr, 54bc, 60bl, 73c, 80bl (Catmando), 7c, 25br, 37b, 40–41 background, 42bl, 43cr, 44bl, 64bl (Herschel Hoffmeyer), 9cr (releon8211), 1tr, 10c, 64–65, 90–91 (Dotted Yeti), 11tr (Nicolas Primola), 14c (nld), 14bc (Valentyna Chukhlyebova), 15tr (Marques), 19tc (Filippo Vanzo), 20c (gorosan), 24b (Lukasz Pawel Szczepanski), 26b, 38b, 45cr, 56–57, 77br (Elenarts), 29br (Lefteris Papaulakis), 31tl (Noiel), 32b (dcwcreations), 37t, 87c, 94t (Evgeniy Mahnyov), 39tr (Natursports), 40cr (Mark Brandon), 47cr, 83bl (topimages), 51cr (DM7), 52b (Wlad74), 55br (Alex Coan), 58bl (Martina Badini), 61t (Akkharat Jarusilawong), 63tr, 93br (Reimar), 65tc (Ton Bangkeaw), 67br (Love Lego), 78bl (Danny Ye), 85cr (Sebastian Kaulitzki), 89tr, 96b (AuntSpray), 90bl (Ivan Smuk), 91tl (Esteban de Armas). All animal silhouettes by Shutterstock.

Front cover, all images: **Shutterstock** (Warpaint). Back cover: **Stefano Azzalin:** tl; **Mat Edwards:** br; **Shutterstock:** bl, (Warpaint), tr (Daniel Eskridge).

ARCTURUS

This edition published in 2021 by Arcturus Publishing Limited
26/27 Bickels Yard, 151–153 Bermondsey Street,
London SE1 3HA

Author: Claudia Martin
Designer: Lorraine Inglis
Consultant: Dougal Dixon
Editors: Becca Clunes and Claudia Martin
Design manager: Jessica Holliland
Editorial manager: Joe Harris

ISBN: 978-1-3988-0250-6

CH007349NT
Supplier 29, Date 0321, Print run 10272

Printed in China

Children's First Dinosaur ENCYCLOPEDIA

CONTENTS

AMAZING DINOSAURS

Millions of years ago, reptiles called dinosaurs walked the Earth. Today's reptiles include lizards and crocodiles, but dinosaurs were larger, fiercer, or stranger than any reptile alive today. From *Tyrannosaurus* to *Diplodocus*, find out about the amazing dinosaurs.

Meat-Eating Dinosaurs

Little meat-eating dinosaurs chased insects or frogs. Big meat-eaters used sharp teeth and claws to kill other dinosaurs, fish, or mammals.

The Asian dinosaur *Ichthyovenator* ate fish and flying reptiles.

Acrocanthosaurus was a meat-eating dinosaur 11 m (36 ft) long.

Plant-Eating Dinosaurs

Plant-eaters fed on leaves, fruits, or nuts. Every plant-eater needed to escape the jaws of meat-eaters. Some ran away fast, while others were too big or spiky to be eaten.

Gigantspinosaurus had long spikes on its shoulders, which made it hard to capture.

Like all dinosaurs, it had four limbs.

Flying and Swimming Reptiles

While dinosaurs stomped or scampered across the land, other reptiles flew through the air on wide wings. In the oceans, swimming reptiles snapped up fish, squid, or each other.

Flying reptiles had wings up to 11 m (36 ft) wide.

5

THE AGE OF DINOSAURS

The first dinosaurs lived 233 million years ago. Over millions of years, around 1,000 species of dinosaurs walked our planet. A species is a group of animals that look very like each other. By around 66 million years ago, all the dinosaurs were gone.

Altirhinus lived between 107 and 100 million years ago.

Changing Earth

Earth's surface is made of giant plates of rock that move slowly on the melted rock lying beneath. Over many millions of years, these moving plates change the shape of the continents.

When the first dinosaurs were alive, all the continents made one supercontinent.

By 5 million years ago, Earth's continents looked as they do today.

North America

Europe

Asia

Africa

Australia

Antarctica

South America

Changing Dinosaurs

Over millions of years, all living things change, growing bigger, smaller, toothier, or hairier. This slow change is called evolution. While new dinosaur species evolved, others died out.

Early plant-eaters were small.

Millions of years later, huge, long-necked plant-eaters had evolved.

Its home was the land we now call Asia.

ALTIRHINUS (al-tee-RY-nus)
HOW BIG: 6 to 7 m (20 to 23 ft) long
HOME: Woodlands in Asia
FOOD: Leaves, fruits, and seeds
WHEN: 107 to 100 million years ago

FINDING FOSSILS

We know about dinosaurs because of fossils. Fossils are the remains of animals and plants that died long ago. We can study a fossil to find out the size and shape of the animal. The place where we find a fossil tells us where the animal lived.

INGENTIA (in-JEN-tee-uh)
HOW BIG: 7 to 10 m (23 to 33 ft) long
HOME: Plains in South America
FOOD: Leaves of shrubs
WHEN: 210 to 205 million years ago

Making Fossils

When an animal dies, its body usually rots away. But if it is quickly buried by sand or mud, its bones, teeth, and horns slowly harden into rock. The sand or mud also turns to rock.

It usually takes thousands of years for a fossil to form.

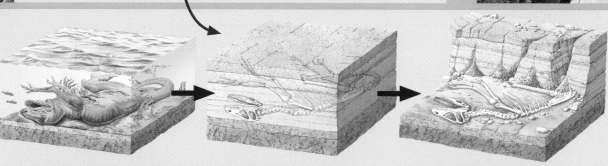

1. A dead dinosaur sinks in a lake, swamp, or sea.

2. Its soft parts rot, but its bones harden.

3. The fossil is found when the rock wears away.

A scientist who studies fossils is called a paleontologist (or palaeontologist).

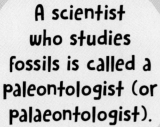

Leaving Clues

Not all fossils are of bodies. Sometimes, a dinosaur's footprints were buried quickly and then hardened into rock. We can also find dinosaurs' eggs, nests, and poop!

The size and distance between a dinosaur's footprints tell us how big its feet and legs were.

This fossil belongs to a dinosaur called *Ingentia*.

LIFE IN WATER

Our planet formed 4.5 billion years ago. For a long time, there was no life on Earth. Then, 3.5 billion years ago, tiny, simple living things appeared in the oceans. Every animal or plant that ever lived—from dinosaurs to humans and trees—evolved from those tiny things.

Earliest Animals

Animals are living things that move, eat other living things, and breathe oxygen in air or water. The first basic animals evolved in the oceans around 665 million years ago.

By around 500 million years ago, there were many different animals in the oceans.

DIPLOCAULUS (dip-lo-COW-lus)
HOW BIG: 80 to 100 cm (31 to 39 in) long
HOME: In and around water in North America and Africa
FOOD: Fish and insects
WHEN: 306 to 255 million years ago

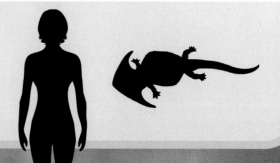

Four Legs

The first four-legged animals evolved in the oceans 370 million years ago. Amphibians were some of the earliest. Amphibians can do something amazing: Although they are born in water, as adults they can breathe air and spend time on land.

All today's animals with four legs—or two legs and two arms or wings—evolved from early four-legged animals like *Crassigyrinus*.

Diplocaulus was an amphibian, like today's frogs.

Its four legs paddled in water and walked on land.

THE FIRST REPTILES

Reptiles were the first four-legged animals to spend all their time on land. The earliest reptiles lived 312 million years ago. Over many millions of years, early reptiles evolved into dinosaurs, lizards, snakes, crocodiles, and turtles.

DIMETRODON (dy-MET-roh-don)
HOW BIG: 2 to 5 m (7 to 16 ft) long
HOME: Swamps in North America and Europe
FOOD: Insects, reptiles, and amphibians
WHEN: 295 to 272 million years ago

Bony spines made a "sail" for showing off to a mate.

The early reptile *Dimetrodon* had sharp teeth for biting prey.

Suited to Land

Reptiles evolved from amphibians. Yet while amphibians needed to stay close to water, reptiles were suited to land. Amphibians had thin skin that must be kept damp, but reptiles had scaly skin. Amphibians laid soft eggs in water, but reptiles laid eggs with shells that did not dry out on land.

Just 25 cm (10 in) long, *Hylonomus* was the earliest known reptile.

Land of Food

Many small land animals were waiting to be eaten by early reptiles, including six-legged insects, many-legged millipedes, and snails. Early reptiles were small, but over time some grew bigger to eat bigger animals.

Up to 6 m (20 ft) long, the reptile *Cotylorhynchus* lived 279 to 272 million years ago.

DIFFERENT DINOSAURS

Dinosaurs were a group of reptiles that evolved around 233 million years ago. Their skeletons had important differences from the bones of other reptiles. These differences gave dinosaurs advantages that made them very successful for millions of years.

Coelophysis was one of the earliest dinosaurs.

Stand Up Straight!

Unlike other reptiles, dinosaurs walked with their back legs beneath their body rather than sprawled to the sides. This meant they could run faster.

A lizard's legs stretch to the sides, but a dinosaur's strong legs are directly beneath its body.

Like all early dinosaurs, it ran on its back legs.

Super Skulls

Dinosaur teeth were fixed deep in their jaws, so they were less likely to fall out when biting prey. Their skulls also had several extra holes that made them lighter but not weaker.

A *Tyrannosaurus* skull had holes in front of and behind its eyes.

COELOPHYSIS (see-loh-FISE-iss)
HOW BIG: 2 to 3 m (7 to 10 ft) long
HOME: Plains in North America and Africa
FOOD: Lizards and other small animals
WHEN: 216 to 196 million years ago

SCALES AND FEATHERS

Early dinosaurs had skin covered by scales. A few million years later, some meat-eating dinosaurs started to grow feathers. Scales and feathers are made of the same hard material that is in human hair and nails. Scales are usually flat, while feathers are long and branching.

Citipati was a feathered dinosaur that could not fly.

Strong Scales

Most dinosaurs had scales. Scales are small plates that grow from skin, protecting it from damage. Scientists have tested fossilized scales to find out what shade they were.

While some dinosaurs were brown or green, others were brightly patterned!

CITIPATI (SIT-ee-PAT-ee)
HOW BIG: 2 to 3 m (7 to 10 ft) long
HOME: Plains in Asia
FOOD: Small animals and plants
WHEN: 75 to 71 million years ago

Longer feathers grew on its tail and arms.

Fantastic Feathers

Early feathered dinosaurs grew short feathers to keep them warm. Eventually, some meat-eaters grew longer, stronger feathers. Some began to use their feathered arms as wings—and slowly evolved into birds!

Birds evolved from feathered, flying dinosaurs like *Microraptor*.

LIFE IN A HERD

The fossils of groups of dinosaurs are often found together, which means that some dinosaurs probably lived in herds. Plant-eating dinosaurs were much safer in a herd. Some meat-eaters might also have hunted, slept, or nested together.

SAUROPOSEIDON
(SORE-oh-puh-SY-don)
HOW BIG: 27 to 34 m (89 to 112 ft) long
HOME: Swamps and plains
in North America
FOOD: Leaves of trees
WHEN: 112 million years ago

Young dinosaurs were safer beside their parents.

Together for Safety

Like a herd of today's deer, a herd of plant-eating dinosaurs could watch out for danger together. When attacked, the herd could confuse meat-eaters by running in all directions.

When the herd is attacked by *Gorgosaurus*, *Parasaurolophus* makes alarm calls to warn of danger.

Up to 18 m (59 ft) tall, *Sauroposeidon* was the tallest known dinosaur.

Competing Together

Like today's male deer, dinosaurs may have competed with others in the herd for leadership, for the best feeding areas, or for finding a mate. They may have fought with their horns or shown off the size of their neck frills.

Around 79 million years ago, two *Diabloceratops* prepare for battle.

LAYING EGGS

Like birds today, dinosaurs laid eggs with a tough shell that kept the growing babies safe until hatching. Eggs were laid in a nest made by scraping a hollow or digging a burrow. Some dinosaurs sat on their eggs to warm them, while others buried their eggs and then left.

Shape and Size

The eggs of plant-eaters were usually round, but meat-eaters' eggs were longer and thinner. The smallest eggs were 4.5 cm (1.8 in) long. The biggest, laid by a large meat-eater, were 60 cm (24 in) long.

These fossilized eggs were laid by a plant-eater.

Oviraptor used its wings to warm its eggs.

Caring or Not

The dinosaurs that sat on their nests also took care of their babies after they were born. However, big plant-eaters would have run out of food near their nests if they stayed around, so their newborn babies had strong legs to find their own food.

Maiasaura (which means "good mother lizard") looked after her babies for at least a year.

OVIRAPTOR (OH-vee-RAP-tuhr)
HOW BIG: 1 to 2 m (3 to 7 ft) long
HOME: Dry plains in Asia
FOOD: Nuts, seeds, and small animals
WHEN: 75 to 71 million years ago

A female *Oviraptor* laid around 15 eggs in a nest.

21

FAST AND SLOW

We can make guesses about how fast dinosaurs walked and ran by looking at their leg bones and measuring their footprints. The fastest dinosaurs could run quicker than any human adult, while the slowest could have been outrun by a child.

Slowest

Large plant-eaters weighed up to 100 tonnes (110 tons), as much as 50 family cars. They had to walk slowly on their four thick legs. Adults had no need to run, as their size kept them safe from meat-eaters.

Brachiosaurus's legs were suited to holding its great weight rather than to sprinting.

VELOCIRAPTOR
(veh-LOSS-ee-rap-tuhr)
HOW BIG: 1 to 2 m (3 to 7 ft) long
HOME: Dry plains in Asia
FOOD: Small reptiles, amphibians, and mammals
WHEN: 75 to 71 million years ago

Small meat-eaters used speed to catch prey.

Fastest

Slim meat-eaters, such as *Gallimimus*, were the fastest runners. They ran on their back legs. Like today's ostrich, their legs were long and muscly. Possibly some could run as fast as ostriches: 72 km (45 miles) an hour.

Gallimimus used its long tail for balance as it ran.

Velociraptor could have reached 40 km (25 miles) per hour.

END OF THE DINOSAURS

Around 66 million years ago, a giant space rock, called an asteroid, hit Earth. The disaster killed all the dinosaurs, along with most other large animals. The only dinosaurs that survived were the small feathered ones which had already evolved into birds.

A few months after the asteroid, plant-eating *torosaurus* looks for food.

Asteroid Crash!

The asteroid, which was 15 km (9 miles) wide, fell into the sea near the coast of North America. The crash sent a cloud of dust into the sky, blocking out all sunlight for up to a year.

The asteroid left a crater 180 km (112 miles) wide.

TOROSAURUS (TOR-oh-SORE-us)
HOW BIG: 8 to 9 m (26 to 30 ft) long
HOME: Woodlands and plains in
North America
FOOD: Leaves of trees and
flowering plants
WHEN: 68 to 66 million years ago

Plants have died,
but their fallen
seeds may
have survived.

No Sunlight

Most plants died from lack of sunlight. Soon
plant-eating dinosaurs ran out of food.
Without the plant-eaters, the meat-eating
dinosaurs could not survive.

A desperate meat-eater feeds on a dead plant-eater,
while flying reptiles wait their turn.

RISE OF THE MAMMALS

Only a quarter of Earth's animals survived the asteroid strike. Among the survivors were little mammals, which ate fallen seeds or worms until the clouds cleared. With the huge, fierce dinosaurs gone, mammals slowly evolved to be many different shapes and sizes.

The woolly mammoth was a relative of today's elephants.

Mammal Time

The first mammals evolved from reptiles around 225 million years ago. Their scales became hair. Instead of laying eggs, they began to give birth to live babies they fed on milk.

Mammals evolved from hairy reptiles like *Lycaenops*, which lived 270 to 251 million years ago.

New and Old

Over the years, new mammals have evolved, then died out. Today's mammals include dogs, cats, and humans. The first dogs evolved 37 million years ago, while cats appeared 25 million years ago. Humans have been around for only 350,000 years.

Smilodon was a big cat that lived from 2.5 million to 10,000 years ago.

WOOLLY MAMMOTH
HOW BIG: 5 to 7 m (16 to 23 ft) long
HOME: Grasslands in North America, Europe, and Asia
FOOD: Grasses, leaves, and mosses
WHEN: 400,000 to 4,000 years ago

Thick hair kept it warm when Earth was colder than it is now.

MEAT-EATING DINOSAURS

Meat-eating dinosaurs had sharp teeth and claws for catching and chewing their food. Some meat-eaters ate dinosaurs, but others ate fish, lizards, or insects. While the biggest, fiercest meat-eaters reached 16 m (52 ft) long, the smallest were only 34 cm (1ft) long.

GIGANOTOSAURUS (jig-an-OH-toe-SORE-us)
HOW BIG: 12 to 13 m (39 to 47 ft) long
HOME: Swamps in South America
FOOD: Plant-eating dinosaurs
WHEN: 98 to 97 million years ago

Most theropods had much shorter front limbs than back limbs.

Dinosaur Diet

Around 233 million years ago, the earliest dinosaurs were meat-eaters. Over millions of years, some dinosaurs evolved (or slowly changed) to eat plants. Of all the dinosaurs we know, around one-third were meat-eaters, while two-thirds were plant-eaters.

Feathery *Anchiornis* was one of the smallest meat-eaters. It ate lizards and fish.

Giganotosaurus's long tail helped it to balance on its back legs.

Theropods

All the meat-eating dinosaurs belonged to a group of similar dinosaurs called theropods. Theropod means "beast foot" in ancient Greek. Theropods walked on their back legs. Most big theropods had scaly skin, but some smaller theropods had feathers.

Like most theropods, *Megaraptor* had three main fingers and three main toes.

DILOPHOSAURUS

Around 193 million years ago, *Dilophosaurus* was the largest meat-eater in North America. Later North American meat-eaters, such as *Tyrannosaurus*, grew much larger. *Dilophosaurus* means "two-crested lizard." It had 33 slim, curving teeth for seizing prey.

Having a Rest

One *Dilophosaurus* left dents in the sand when it was resting. The sand was baked hard by the sun, then covered by more sand. The dents stayed in the sandstone rock as it formed.

The dents showed us how *Dilophosaurus* held its hands, with the palms facing each other.

Dilophosaurus weighed the same as a modern horse.

It tore at prey with its long, narrow jaws.

Showing Off

Dilophosaurus's skull bones formed two crests. The crest bones were too thin to be strong enough for fighting, so the crests were probably for display. Males may have shown them off to attract females.

The crest bones were covered by tough horn and skin, making the crest taller.

DILOPHOSAURUS (dy-LOFF-oh-SORE-us)
HOW BIG: 6 to 7 m (20 to 23 ft) long
HOME: Around water in North America
FOOD: Fish and small land animals
WHEN: 193 million years ago

ALLOSAURUS

This large meat-eater had up to 44 sharp teeth with jagged edges. These teeth sometimes fell out as *Allosaurus* ripped through flesh, so they are common fossils. *Allosaurus* bite marks have been found in dinosaurs as large as *Stegosaurus*.

Its short horns might have been helpful for bashing other *Allosauruses*.

Killer Claws

Each hand had three fingers, armed with long, curved claws. *Allosaurus* could not reach forward easily with its short arms. However, once prey was in its mouth, the hook-like claws stopped escape.

An *Allosaurus* claw could grow over 18 cm (7 in) long.

ALLOSAURUS (AL-oh-SORE-us)
HOW BIG: 8 to 12 m (26 to 39 ft) long
HOME: Forests and plains in North
America and Europe
FOOD: Large plant-eating dinosaurs
WHEN: 155 to 145 million years ago

Growing Up

Allosaurus reached its full size by around 15 years old. Every year as it grew, it gained around 150 kg (330 lb)—the weight of 40 human babies. Most *Allosauruses* lived to be around 25.

Allosaurus was big enough to attack young or sick Diplodocuses.

Allosaurus may have worked in a team to hunt big prey.

33

CERATOSAURUS

Ceratosaurus means "horn lizard." This medium-sized meat-eater had a horn on its snout and a pair of horns over its eyes. These small horns were possibly not useful weapons, but may have helped a *Ceratosaurus* recognize other *Ceratosauruses*.

Competing Dinosaurs

Ceratosaurus lived in the same area at the same time as *Allosaurus*. To avoid competing with the bigger dinosaur for food, *Ceratosaurus* may often have fed on water-living animals.

Ceratosaurus waded into swamps and lakes to catch fish.

CERATOSAURUS (keh-RAT-oh-SORE-us)
HOW BIG: 5 to 7 m (16 to 23 ft) long
HOME: Swamps and plains in North America
FOOD: Fish, crocodiles, and turtles
WHEN: 153 to 148 million years ago

34

A line of small bony plates ran down its back.

Ceratosaurus's teeth were long and blade-like.

Hollow Bones

Like other meat-eaters, *Ceratosaurus* had bones that were hollow. This made them lighter and more likely to bend than break in a fall. Birds, which evolved from meat-eating dinosaurs, also have hollow bones.

Unlike most meat-eaters, *Ceratosaurus* had four fingers on each hand.

SPINOSAURUS

Spinosaurus was one of the biggest meat-eaters that ever lived. Its long, narrow skull looked rather like a modern crocodile's. This dinosaur used the long claws on its thumbs, as well as its sharp teeth, to grab slippery fish.

Spinosaurus's teeth grew up to 15 cm (6 in) long.

SPINOSAURUS (SPINE-oh-SORE-us)
HOW BIG: 12 to 16 m (39 to 52 ft) long
HOME: Around water in North Africa
FOOD: Fish, dinosaurs, and flying reptiles
WHEN: 112 to 93 million years ago

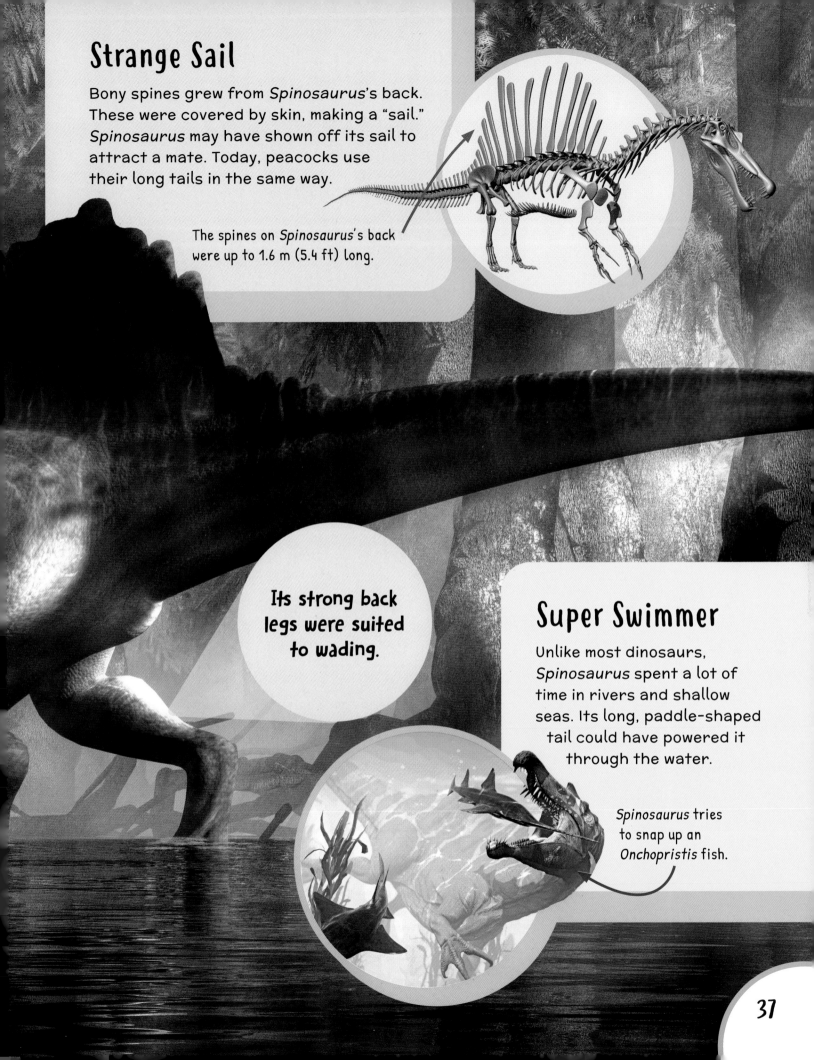

Strange Sail

Bony spines grew from *Spinosaurus*'s back. These were covered by skin, making a "sail." *Spinosaurus* may have shown off its sail to attract a mate. Today, peacocks use their long tails in the same way.

The spines on *Spinosaurus*'s back were up to 1.6 m (5.4 ft) long.

Its strong back legs were suited to wading.

Super Swimmer

Unlike most dinosaurs, *Spinosaurus* spent a lot of time in rivers and shallow seas. Its long, paddle-shaped tail could have powered it through the water.

Spinosaurus tries to snap up an *Onchopristis* fish.

COMPSOGNATHUS

This delicate little dinosaur lived on islands of the Tethys Sea, in what is now France and Germany. It had a very long tail, which helped it balance as it raced and swerved after fast-running prey. *Compsognathus* means "dainty jaw" in ancient Greek.

Lizard Lover

We know what *Compsognathus* ate because one of its fossils had the remains of its last meal inside its stomach. This *Compsognathus* had gulped down a small, long-tailed lizard.

Like modern lizards, *Compsognathus*'s lizard prey could scuttle fast.

Large eyes helped *Compsognathus* to spot prey.

Slim and Speedy

Compsognathus was built for speed, with long legs and a slim, light skeleton. Its neck and jaws were also long, so it could snatch prey as it tried to hide under rocks or plants.

In this fossil, *Compsognathus*'s head and neck are bent round, over its back.

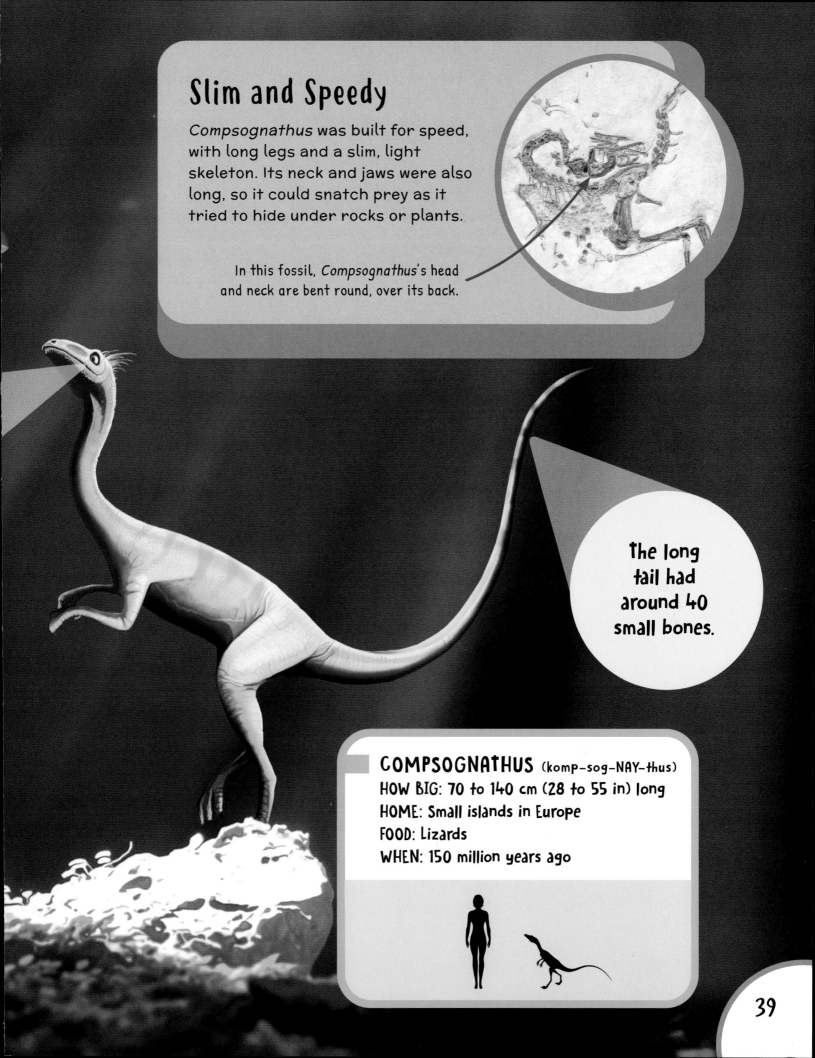

The long tail had around 40 small bones.

COMPSOGNATHUS (komp-sog-NAY-thus)
HOW BIG: 70 to 140 cm (28 to 55 in) long
HOME: Small islands in Europe
FOOD: Lizards
WHEN: 150 million years ago

39

DEINONYCHUS

Deinonychus gets its name (meaning "terrible claw" in ancient Greek) from the extra-long claw on the second toe of each foot. These dangerous toe claws were used for holding struggling prey on the ground, while Deinonychus bit with its 70 sharp teeth.

Feathery Family

No feathered fossils have been found of Deinonychus. However, scientists think it was feathered because they know that its close relatives had long, thick feathers.

In this fossil of Deinonychus's relative Microraptor, feathers can be seen on its arms, legs, and tail.

The longest claw was held off the ground when walking.

Preferred Prey

Scientists think *Deinonychus* liked to eat the plant-eater *Tenontosaurus* as their fossils are often found together. Adult *Tenontosauruses* were bigger than *Deinonychus*, so the meat-eater may only have eaten babies.

Packs of hungry *Deinonychus* could have attacked a young *Tenontosaurus* together.

DEINONYCHUS (dy-NON-ik-us)
HOW BIG: 2 to 3 m (7 to 10 ft) long
HOME: Swamps and plains in North America
FOOD: Plant-eating dinosaurs
WHEN: 115 to 108 million years ago

Feathers kept *Deinonychus* warm but it could not fly.

TYRANNOSAURUS

Tyrannosaurus was the biggest meat-eater that ever lived in North America. An adult *Tyrannosaurus* had no need to fear any other animal. However, this deadly beast was wiped out when a giant space rock hit Earth, around 66 million years ago.

Powerful Bite

Tyrannosaurus had one of the strongest bites of any animal that has lived. Its bite force was equal to the weight of three small cars. Its thick, strong jaw bones could open very wide, before powerful muscles snapped them closed.

Tyrannosaurus's jaws crushed bone.

TYRANNOSAURUS (ty-RAN-oh-SORE-us)
HOW BIG: 11 to 12 m (36 to 40 ft) long
HOME: Swamps and forests in North America
FOOD: Plant-eating dinosaurs, found alive or already dead
WHEN: 68 to 66 million years ago

Tyrannosaurus's knife-like teeth grew over 30 cm (12 in) long.

Sense of Smell

Like modern meat-eaters, from great white sharks to wolves, *Tyrannosaurus* had a very good sense of smell. The part of its brain that made sense of smells was also large.

Tyrannosaurus's sense of smell enabled it to track plant-eating dinosaurs for many miles.

The short arms had only two clawed fingers.

DEINOCHEIRUS

Although *Deinocheirus* was part of the theropod group of meat-eaters, it fed on plants as well as on small animals. The dinosaur's large claws earned it the name *Deinocheirus*, which means "horrible hand." Yet the claws were blunt and probably used only for digging up plants.

The tail ended in a fan of feathers.

Scary Sail

On its back, *Deinocheirus* had bony spines that made a "sail." The sail made *Deinocheirus* look bigger to meat-eaters thinking of an attack.

In hot weather, the sail helped *Deinocheirus* cool down, as it gave more skin surface to lose heat from.

Duck Face

Deinocheirus's jaws were shaped like the beak of a duck. Just as ducks do today, it may have used its toothless beak for probing underwater for plants, small fish, insects, and worms.

Fish scales have been found inside *Deinocheirus*'s stomach.

Its unusually long arms could reach high and low for plants.

DEINOCHEIRUS (dee-EN-oh-SHARE-us)
HOW BIG: 8 to 12 m (26 to 39 ft) long
HOME: Around water in Asia
FOOD: Small animals and plants
WHEN: 71 to 69 million years ago

CAUDIPTERYX

With its small body, feathers, and beak, *Caudipteryx* looked very like a bird. However, its arms were not fully developed into wings: They were not long and strong enough to let *Caudipteryx* fly. The earliest birds were relatives of *Caudipteryx*.

Two meat-eating *Dilongs* have spotted little *Caudipteryx*.

Tail Feather

Caudipteryx means "tail feather" in ancient Greek. This dinosaur's tail had a fan of feathers. Feathers on the tail and arms helped to keep eggs warm when sitting on a nest.

Like a modern peacock, a male *Caudipteryx* may have shown off its tail to attract females.

Stone Swallower

Like some birds, *Caudipteryx* swallowed stones. These ground up tough plants in a special, extra stomach called a gizzard. The gizzard walls had strong muscles that squeezed the food and stones.

Stones can be seen in the stomach of this *Caudipteryx* fossil.

Caudipteryx's beak held a few small, weak teeth.

CAUDIPTERYX (kaw-DIP-tuh-riks)
HOW BIG: 70 to 80 cm
  (28 to 31 in) long
HOME: Around water in Asia
FOOD: Small animals and plants
WHEN: 125 million years ago

ARCHAEOPTERYX

Over millions of years, some dinosaurs grew to look more and more like birds. By 150 million years ago, dinosaurs like *Archaeopteryx* could use their feathered arms to make short flights. By 130 million years ago, the first true birds had evolved from their dinosaur grandparents.

Dinosaur or Bird?

Archaeopteryx had features of both dinosaurs and birds. Like most dinosaurs but unlike modern birds, it had teeth. However, its arm muscles and bones had evolved into wide wings.

Archaeoptyerx used its sharp little teeth for snapping insects.

Its bony tail was much longer than a modern bird's.

ARCHAEOPTERYX (ARK-ee-OPT-er-ix)
HOW BIG: 30 to 50 cm (12 to 20 in) long
HOME: Islands in Europe
FOOD: Insects and other small animals
WHEN: 150 to 148 million years ago

Unlike today's birds, Archaeopteryx had clawed fingers.

Dinosaurs Are Alive!

After a space rock hit Earth 66 million years ago, all the dinosaurs died out—apart from the dinosaurs that had evolved into birds. Today's birds are the closest living relatives of *Tyrannosaurus*.

Hesperornis was a toothed bird that lived 83 to 78 million years ago.

PLANT-EATING DINOSAURS

The biggest plant-eaters were 40 m (131 ft) long, but the littlest were dog-sized. Some walked on two legs and others on four. Many had long necks, but others had bony plates. Plant-eaters developed different body shapes to find food and defend themselves against hungry meat-eaters.

Kosmoceratops had more horns than any animal that ever lived.

Telling Teeth

Fossils of plant-eaters' teeth tell us what they ate. Some dinosaurs had thin teeth for stripping soft fern leaves. Others had wide, spoon-shaped teeth for ripping tough twigs.

Edmontosaurus had a hard toothless beak for clipping stems, plus hundreds of small teeth at the back of its mouth for grinding.

It cut through stems with its hard, horny beak.

Precious Plant-Eaters

More dinosaurs ate plants than ate meat. Today, there are more plant-eating animals than meat-eaters, too. If there were more meat-eaters, there would soon be no animals left for them to eat!

A pack of meat-eaters corners a frightened plant-eating *Einiosaurus*.

KOSMOCERATOPS (KOZ-mo-SEH-ra-tops)
HOW BIG: 4 to 5 m (13 to 16 ft) long
HOME: Forests in North America
FOOD: Woody plants
WHEN: 76 to 75 million years ago

DIPLODOCUS

The huge size of this peaceful dinosaur protected it from attack. Even the largest local meat-eaters, *Allosaurus* and *Ceratosaurus*, could not kill an adult *Diplodocus*. This dinosaur was part of the sauropod group of plant-eaters, which had long necks and long tails.

Diplodocus's neck was over 6 m (20 ft) long.

Feeding High and Low

Its long neck enabled *Diplodocus* to feed on low plants a distance away, saving the energy needed to walk toward them. It could also rear up on its back legs to reach branches up to 11 m (36 ft) high.

Diplodocus's long neck meant it did not have to compete with most other plant-eaters for food.

DIPLODOCUS (dip-LOH-doh-kus)
HOW BIG: 24 to 32 m (79 to 105 ft) long
HOME: Plains in North America
FOOD: Soft leaves
WHEN: 154 to 152 million years ago

Cracking a Whip

Diplodocus's tail grew to 14 m (46 ft) long. Made of 80 small bones, it was very bendy. The dinosaur could crack it like a whip, making a suddenloud noise that frightened away predators.

Diplodocus's tail was longer than the longest buses.

Four thick legs supported its 18-tonne (20-ton) weight.

ARGENTINOSAURUS

Argentinosaurus was probably the biggest land animal that ever lived. It reached over 39 m (128 ft) long, which is longer than eight cars. Like *Diplodocus*, *Argentinosaurus* was a long-necked, long-tailed sauropod. It was one of the slowest moving of all the dinosaurs.

Staying Safe

Fossilized footprints show us sauropods often moved in herds. Young dinosaurs walked in the middle to stay safe from attack. It took around 30 years for a newborn *Argentinosaurus*, just 1 m (3 ft) long, to reach full size.

Argentinosaurus herds may have migrated in search of food and water.

54

Argentinosaurus's skin was covered by small scales.

Its skull was small enough to be held up by the slim neck.

ARGENTINOSAURUS
(AR–juhn–TEE–no–SORE–us)
HOW BIG: 30 to 39 m (98 to 128 ft) long
HOME: Plains in South America
FOOD: Leaves of conifer trees
WHEN: 96 to 92 million years ago

Wait for It...

This dinosaur's size gave room for a huge stomach and long intestines, which are tubes where food is broken down. It took two weeks for plants to travel through this dinosaur, giving extra time to soak up their goodness.

Fossilized dinosaur poop is called coprolite.

IGUANODON

In 1825, soon after its fossils were first found, this dinosaur was named *Iguanodon* (meaning "iguana tooth" in ancient Greek). Its teeth were like those of modern plant-eating lizards called iguanas. *Iguanodon* was not huge, but it could use its thumb spikes to defend itself.

Iguanodon's 108 teeth were replaced when they fell out.

Thumb Spike

Iguanodon's thumbs had long, pointed claws. These could stab an attacker, but may also have opened fruit and seeds.

As well as a thumb claw, *Iguanodon* had a long, bendable fifth finger for grasping food.

IGUANODON (ig-WAH-noh-don)
HOW BIG: 9 to 13 m (30 to 43 ft) long
HOME: Forests and plains in Europe
FOOD: Leaves, fruits, and nuts
WHEN: 126 to 122 million years ago

Horny Beak

The fronts of *Iguanodon*'s jaws were toothless but pointed, forming a beak. Like the beaks of birds and other plant-eating dinosaurs, *Iguanodon*'s beak was covered in horn, making it strong and sharp.

The horn of *Iguanodon*'s beak was made of keratin, which is also in animals' claws, horns, and scales—and human nails.

Light, young *Iguanodons* walked on their back legs.

PARASAUROLOPHUS

This plant-eater lived in herds in North America. Together, the herd could watch for danger in all directions. When searching for leaves, *Parasaurolophus* strolled on all fours. When it needed to escape danger, it ran fast on its back legs.

Duck Bill

This dinosaur had long, flat jaw bones, making its mouth a little like a duck's bill. *Parasaurolophus* clipped off twigs with its hard jaws, then mashed food with the teeth at the back of its mouth.

Parasaurolophus and its relatives are often called duckbilled dinosaurs.

the fingers were joined by flesh and skin, making a tough pad.

Noisy Crest

Parasaurolophus had a long, hollow crest on its head. This made the dinosaur's calls louder. In the same way, the tubes of a trumpet enable its player to make really loud sounds.

Parasaurolophus could call to other members of its herd from far away.

A stiff tail helped *Parasaurolophus* to balance on its back legs.

PARASAUROLOPHUS (PA-ra-sore-OL-off-us)
HOW BIG: 7 to 9.5 m (23 to 31 ft) long
HOME: Plains in North America
FOOD: Tough plants
WHEN: 76 to 73 million years ago

PSITTACOSAURUS

With a round skull and large beak, this dinosaur's head looked like a parrot's. This earned *Psittacosaurus* its name, which means "parrot lizard." Its lower jaw could be pulled back inside the upper jaw, then opened and closed like a nutcracker to smash nuts and seeds.

Psittacosaurus could smell predators at a distance.

Big Brain

Plant-eaters usually had smaller brains than meat-eaters because it takes less brain power to see plants than to track moving prey. However, the size and shape of *Psittacosaurus*'s brain tell us it was fairly quick thinking and had good senses.

Animals with bigger brains often spend longer caring for their babies.

Big Eyes

Psittacosaurus had large eye sockets, so it must have had big eyes. Big eyes help an animal see well in poor light. *Psittacosaurus* may have looked for food in short bursts through the day and night.

Although eyeballs are not usually fossilized, eye sockets show the size of the eye.

It may have shown off its bristles to attract a mate.

PSITTACOSAURUS (SIT-ak-oh-SORE-us)
HOW BIG: 1 to 2 m (3 to 7 ft) long
HOME: Forests in Asia
FOOD: Nuts, seeds, and leaves
WHEN: 126 to 101 million years ago

PACHYCEPHALOSAURUS

The name of this dinosaur means "thick-headed lizard." *Pachycephalosaurus's* spiky skull was unusually thick and dome shaped. This dinosaur walked on its back legs, balancing the weight of its heavy head with its long, stiff tail.

Head Banger

These dinosaurs may have used their heads to batter each other in fights over mates or feeding places. Their strong skulls, up to 25 cm (10 in) thick, protected their tiny brains from injury.

A *Pachycephalosaurus* rams a rival in the side using its head.

PACHYCEPHALOSAURUS
(pak-ee-SEF-ah-lo-SORE-us)
HOW BIG: 4 to 5 m (13 to 16 ft) long
HOME: Forests in North America
FOOD: Leaves and small animals
WHEN: 70 to 66 million years ago

Tooth Clues

Pachycephalosaurus's teeth give clues it had a mixed diet. Its tiny back teeth could only have ripped soft leaves. However, its longer, sharper front teeth were shaped like a meat-eater's. These could have pierced insects and other small animals.

Pachycephalosaurus's delicate teeth tell us it did not eat tough, woody plants.

Large, forward-facing eyes were quick to spot prey or predators.

Its bulky body easily pushed past branches.

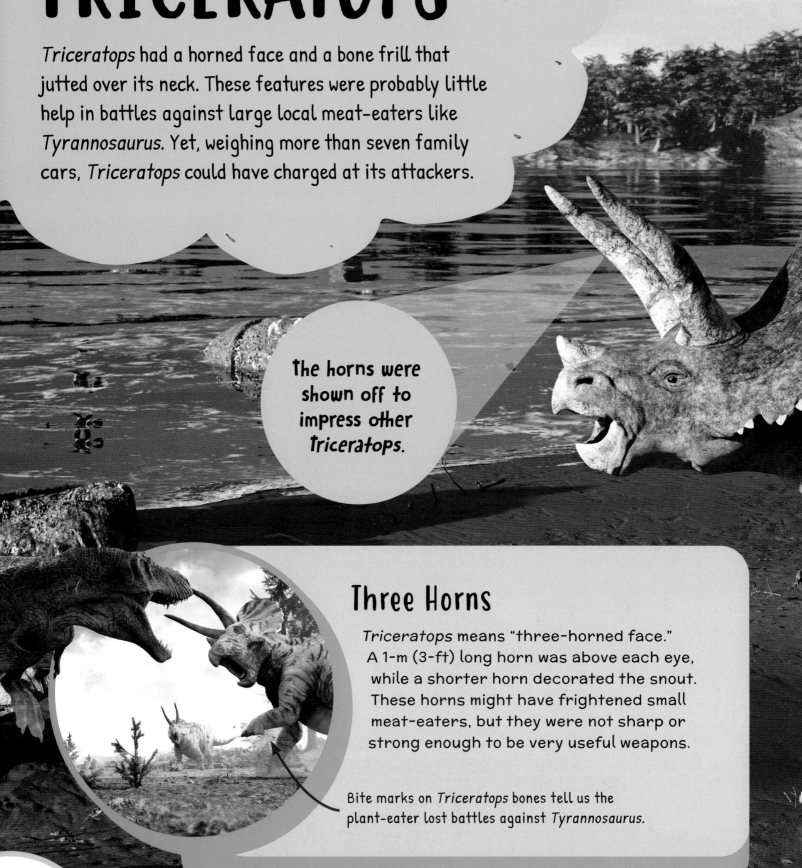

TRICERATOPS

Triceratops had a horned face and a bone frill that jutted over its neck. These features were probably little help in battles against large local meat-eaters like *Tyrannosaurus*. Yet, weighing more than seven family cars, *Triceratops* could have charged at its attackers.

The horns were shown off to impress other *triceratops*.

Three Horns

Triceratops means "three-horned face." A 1-m (3-ft) long horn was above each eye, while a shorter horn decorated the snout. These horns might have frightened small meat-eaters, but they were not sharp or strong enough to be very useful weapons.

Bite marks on *Triceratops* bones tell us the plant-eater lost battles against *Tyrannosaurus*.

Weighing In

With its great weight, *Triceratops* could not reach high to feed. Yet it may have used its weight and horns to knock over shrubs and trees. It gripped plants with its hard beak, then mashed them with its back teeth.

Triceratops's skull, up to 2.5 m (8.2 ft) long, was among the largest of all land animals.

Its four broad toes were shaped like hooves.

TRICERATOPS (try-SEH-ra-tops)
HOW BIG: 8 to 9 m (26 to 30 ft) long
HOME: Forests and plains in North America
FOOD: Tough plants
WHEN: 68 to 66 million years ago

STEGOSAURUS

This plant-eater had two rows of kite-shaped plates down its back. Their pattern may have helped *Stegosaurus* recognize other members of its herd from a distance. *Stegosaurus* had a small brain, suiting this dinosaur to a slow and simple life.

STEGOSAURUS (STEG-oh-SORE-us)
HOW BIG: 7 to 9 m (23 to 30 ft) long
HOME: Forest and plains in
North America and Europe
FOOD: Low plants
WHEN: 155 to 150 million years ago

The tail spikes were up to 90 cm (35 in) long.

Terrible Thagomizer

The tip of *Stegosaurus*'s tail had four sharp spikes. When whipped at an attacker, these made deep wounds. This type of tail was named a thagomizer by a cartoonist named Gary Larson.

With a flick of its tail, a stegosaur escapes.

The plates were too thin to protect *Stegosaurus*.

Scales vs. Plates

Unlike scales, which grow from the top layer of an animal's skin, *Stegosaurus*'s back plates grew from deep in its skin. Scales are made from keratin, like claws, while plates are made from bone.

Stegosaurus's biggest plates were 60 cm (24 in) tall

BOREALOPELTA

The first fossil of *Borealopelta* was discovered in 2011. This amazing fossil shows exactly how *Borealopelta's* plates were arranged. Most fossils show only the hard body parts, but this fossil kept the skin. The animal probably drowned, got washed out to sea, then was quickly buried by sand.

Tests on *Borealopelta's* skin show it was reddish brown.

Knobbed Lizards

Borealopelta belonged to a group of plant-eaters called nodosaurs, which means "knobbed lizards" in ancient Greek. Their bodies were protected from teeth and claws by rows of bony plates and spikes.

The nodosaur *Gargoyleosaurus* had thick plates on its back and spikes on its sides.

BOREALOPELTA
(BOH-ree-AH-loh-PEL-tuh)
HOW BIG: 5 to 6 m (16 to 20 ft) long
HOME: Forests in North America
FOOD: Leaves, stems, and twigs
WHEN: 110 million years ago

Stand Firm

Borealopelta's underside was not covered by plates. When attacked, it needed to keep its balance to avoid being rolled over. This effort was helped by its short legs and wide body.

In a battle with *Acrocanthosaurus*, *Borealopelta* tries to stand firm.

The longest spikes were on its shoulders.

ANKYLOSAURUS

Ankylosaurus's heavy plates and short legs made it a slow mover. This tank-like dinosaur was a close relative of the nodosaurs. Yet Ankylosaurus had a terrifying weapon that nodosaurs did not possess: a hard, heavy club at the end of its tail.

Tail Swinger

Ankylosaurus's tail club was made of solid bone. It weighed up to 50 kg (110lb), as much as a 15-year-old human. By swinging its tail, Ankylosaurus could break the leg bones of an attacker.

Even a large meat-eater, such as Tyrannosaurus, could be driven away by a swing of the tail.

the biggest plates were 35 cm (14 in) wide.

Strong Skull

Ankylosaurus means "joined lizard." The bones in this dinosaur's skull were joined together, making it very strong. Extra, flat bones covered the top of the head like tiles.

The skull had an almost triangular shape.

It had four backward-pointing horns.

ANKYLOSAURUS (an-KIH-loh-SORE-us)
HOW BIG: 6 to 8 m (20 to 26 ft) long
HOME: Forests in North America
FOOD: Leaves and fruits
WHEN: 68 to 66 million years ago

71

FLYING AND SWIMMING REPTILES

The first reptiles lived on land, but over millions of years some took to the air or water. Their arms evolved into wings or flippers so they could fly or swim. These flyers and swimmers were not dinosaurs, but they could be just as fierce and deadly.

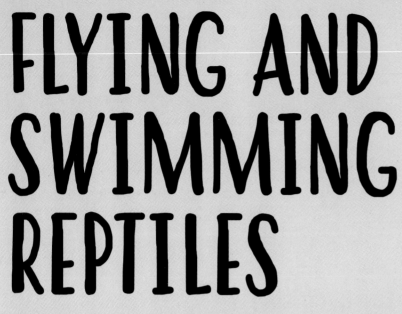

TYLOSAURUS (tile-oh-SORE-us)
HOW BIG: 12 to 14 m (39 to 46 ft) long
HOME: Inland seas in North America
FOOD: Sharks, reptiles, and birds
WHEN: 90 to 66 million years ago

Tylosaurus had gristle between its finger bones, making flippers.

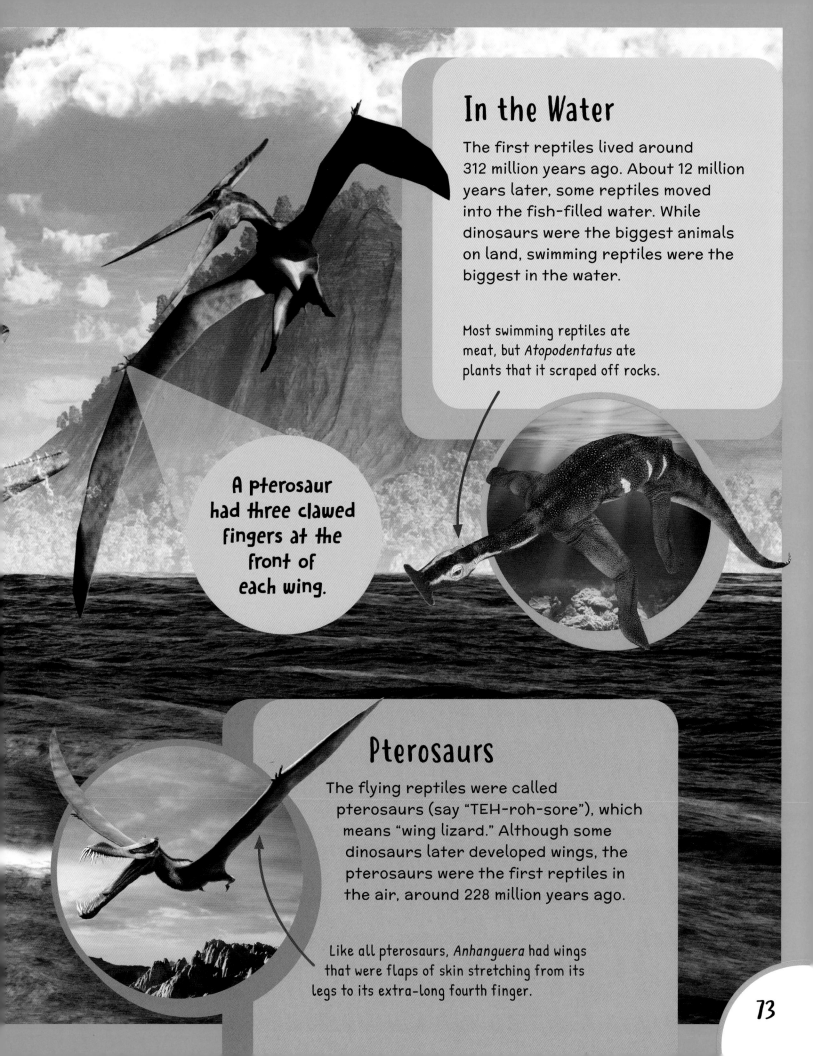

In the Water

The first reptiles lived around 312 million years ago. About 12 million years later, some reptiles moved into the fish-filled water. While dinosaurs were the biggest animals on land, swimming reptiles were the biggest in the water.

Most swimming reptiles ate meat, but *Atopodentatus* ate plants that it scraped off rocks.

A pterosaur had three clawed fingers at the front of each wing.

Pterosaurs

The flying reptiles were called pterosaurs (say "TEH-roh-sore"), which means "wing lizard." Although some dinosaurs later developed wings, the pterosaurs were the first reptiles in the air, around 228 million years ago.

Like all pterosaurs, *Anhanguera* had wings that were flaps of skin stretching from its legs to its extra-long fourth finger.

73

TUPANDACTYLUS

This pterosaur had a large crest on its head made of bone, horn, and skin. Its hard, sharp-edged beak was toothless. Fossils of *Tupandactylus* have been found in Brazil. It was named after the thunder god of the Tupi people, who live in Brazil's Amazon rain forest.

Crest Signals

Like today's crested birds, *Tupandactylus* probably used its crest to signal to other members of its flock. Signals could have been warnings of danger, threats to rivals, or greetings to mates.

Fossils show the shape of the crest bones, but we can make different guesses about the shape and shade of the skin between the bones.

A pterosaur's body was covered in hair-like fuzz for warmth.

Tree Climber

Tupandactylus and its close relatives had curved claws, which would have been useful for holding on to tree branches. Their large beaks were suited to grabbing tree fruits and nuts.

The smaller-crested *Sinopterus* was a close relative of *Tupandactylus*.

TUPANDACTYLUS (too-pan-DAK-till-us)
HOW BIG: 2 to 3 m (7 to 10 ft) long
HOME: Forests in South America
FOOD: Fruits, nuts, and small animals
WHEN: 112 million years ago

The soles of *Tupandactylus*'s feet were scaly.

PTERANODON

Pteranodon's wings were up to 7 m (23 ft) wide, twice as wide as any modern bird's. Broad wings meant *Pteranodon* could glide for long distances without needing to flap. This saved energy as it flew over the ocean in search of fish.

Pteranodon's tall crest was used for attracting a mate.

Fish Eater

Pteranodon scooped up fish using its long, sharp beak. Food was swallowed whole, as this reptile had no teeth for chewing.

We know *Pteranodon* ate fish because fish bones have been found in its stomach.

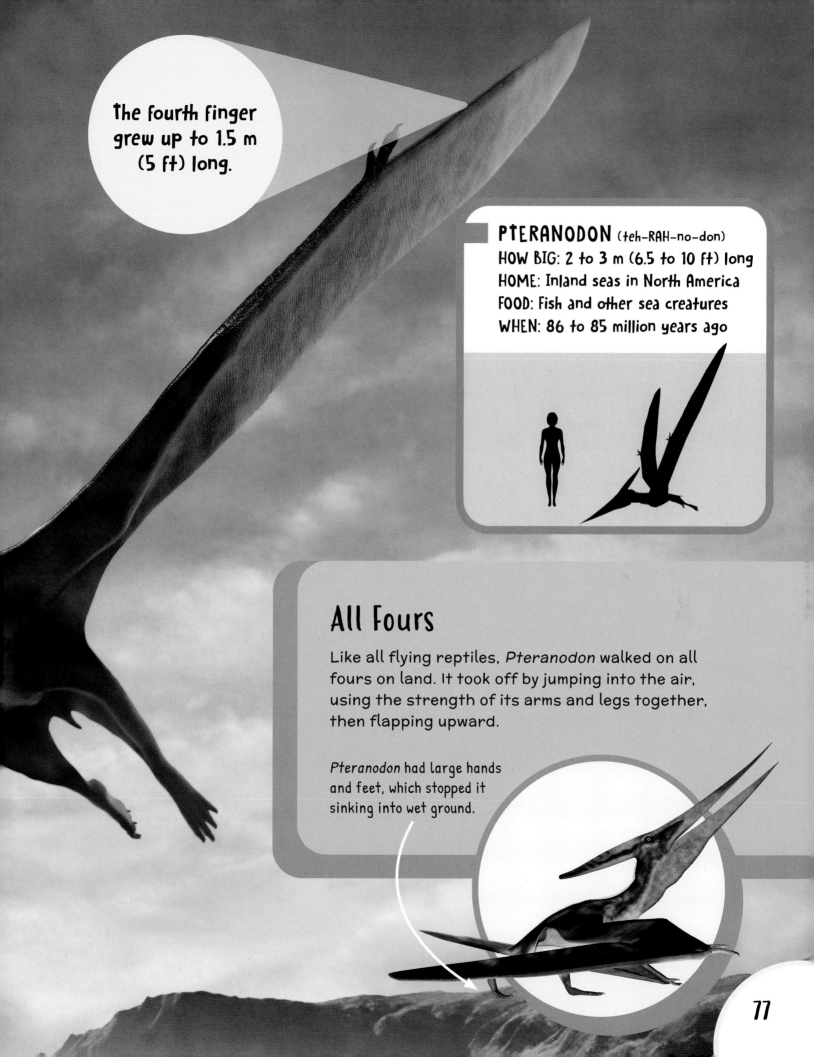

the fourth finger grew up to 1.5 m (5 ft) long.

PTERANODON (teh-RAH-no-don)
HOW BIG: 2 to 3 m (6.5 to 10 ft) long
HOME: Inland seas in North America
FOOD: Fish and other sea creatures
WHEN: 86 to 85 million years ago

All Fours

Like all flying reptiles, *Pteranodon* walked on all fours on land. It took off by jumping into the air, using the strength of its arms and legs together, then flapping upward.

Pteranodon had large hands and feet, which stopped it sinking into wet ground.

QUETZALCOATLUS

Quetzalcoatlus was the largest pterosaur and the largest flying animal ever known to live. It was named after Quetzalcoatl, the feathered serpent god of the Aztecs, a people who lived in Central America in the 14th and 15th centuries.

Stabbing Beak

Quetzalcoatlus had a very long, sharp beak. Together with the pterosaur's long neck, this would have been useful for stabbing and grabbing small animals that tried to run or hide.

The beak had no teeth, but was edged with hard horn.

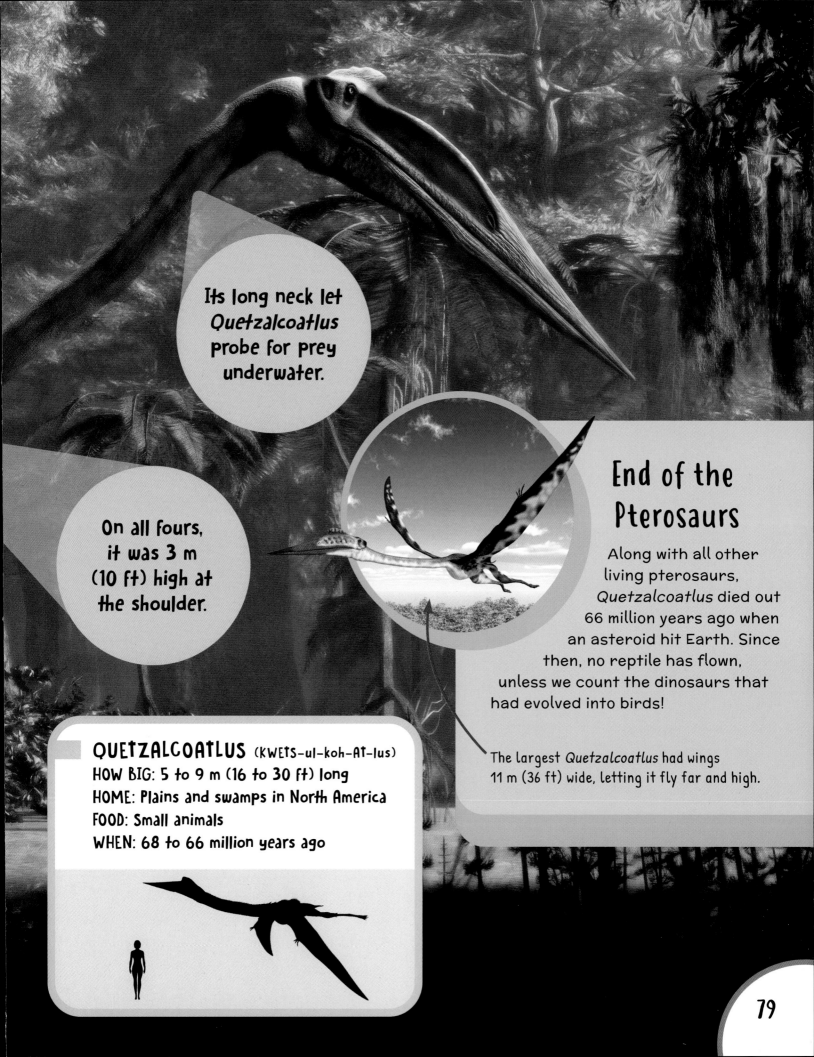

Its long neck let *Quetzalcoatlus* probe for prey underwater.

On all fours, it was 3 m (10 ft) high at the shoulder.

End of the Pterosaurs

Along with all other living pterosaurs, *Quetzalcoatlus* died out 66 million years ago when an asteroid hit Earth. Since then, no reptile has flown, unless we count the dinosaurs that had evolved into birds!

The largest *Quetzalcoatlus* had wings 11 m (36 ft) wide, letting it fly far and high.

QUETZALCOATLUS (KWETS-ul-koh-AT-lus)
HOW BIG: 5 to 9 m (16 to 30 ft) long
HOME: Plains and swamps in North America
FOOD: Small animals
WHEN: 68 to 66 million years ago

PSEPHODERMA

This swimming reptile had thick rounded teeth for crushing shellfish. *Psephoderma* means "pebbly skin" in ancient Greek. Its skin was protected by small scales and larger, thicker bony plates. These plates formed a shell, called a carapace, over its body.

PSEPHODERMA (see-foe-DERM-uh)
HOW BIG: 160 to 180 cm
  (63 to 71 in) long
HOME: Shallow seas in Europe
FOOD: Shellfish
WHEN: 210 million years ago

Needing Protection

Psephoderma belonged to a group of reptiles called placodonts. Early placodonts did not have shells. As other swimming reptiles became sharper toothed, the placodonts grew more bony plates. Late placodonts looked like turtles, but the two groups are not close relatives.

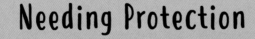

Placodus was an early placodont with no bony plates.

The shell was in two parts, over its rear and over its back.

Breathing Air

Like all swimming reptiles, *Psephoderma* had to go to the surface to breathe air. Weighed down by its plates, it stayed in shallow water so it could surface without getting too tired.

Like *Psephoderma*, *Henodus* was a late placodont that fed on shallow seabeds.

Using its long beak, it felt for shellfish on the seafloor.

ELASMOSAURUS

Long-necked *Elasmosaurus* powered through the ocean using its four large flippers. Its body was so well suited to life in the water that it could not climb ashore. Unlike land-living reptiles, which laid eggs on land, *Elasmosaurus* gave birth to live babies in the water.

Elasmosaurus's neck grew to over 7 m (23 ft) long.

ELASMOSAURUS (eh-LAZZ-moh-SORE-us)
HOW BIG: 10 to 13 m (33 to 43 ft) long
HOME: Inland seas in North America
FOOD: Fish and other small animals
WHEN: 80 million years ago

Surprising Neck

Elasmosaurus could use its long neck to surprise fish, by creeping its head forward to snap them up. This reptile may also have scooped up worms and shellfish from the seabed using its neck like a rake.

Although *Elasmosaurus* has been caught by its neck, its strong body is out of the octopus's reach.

Its smooth flippers were no use for walking on land.

Gripping Teeth

Elasmosaurus had long, sharp teeth for gripping slippery fish. However, it had no chewing teeth, so swallowed prey whole. It may have swallowed stones to mush food in its stomach.

When the mouth was closed, the teeth interlocked, forming a cage from which fish could not escape.

83

KRONOSAURUS

This huge hunter weighed up to 12 tonnes (13 tons), as much as six family cars. It was an apex predator, which means that no other predator was large enough to attack. *Kronosaurus* was named after the powerful Greek god Kronos.

Its massive skull grew up to 285 cm (112 in) long.

Reptile Eater

Kronosaurus had cone-shaped teeth up to 30 cm (12 in) long. Its crocodile-like jaws could open wide—and snap shut hard. This meant it could crush to death other swimming reptiles.

Kronosaurus ate ichthyosaurs and other swimming reptiles.

the body was smoothly shaped to slide easily through water.

Strong Swimmer

The bones and muscles of this reptile's flippers and joints were very strong. *Kronosaurus* was able to push hard against the water with its flippers, reaching a top speed of 10 km (6 miles) an hour.

It swam faster than the quickest human swimmer.

KRONOSAURUS (CRONE-oh-SORE-us)
HOW BIG: 9 to 11 m (30 to 36 ft) long
HOME: Inland seas in Australia and South America
FOOD: Swimming reptiles
WHEN: 120 to 100 million years ago

STENOPTERYGIUS

Stenopterygius had a strong, smoothly shaped body like a modern dolphin's. These very different animals developed the same body shape because it is perfect for fast swimming. *Stenopterygius* swam by wiggling its tail and paddling its flippers.

Dark and Light

Tests on fossilized *Stenopterygius* skin show its stomach was paler than its back. This helped with camouflage. From below, the reptile looked pale against the sunlight shining down through the water. From above, it looked dark against the lightless depths.

This reptile's camouflage helped with hunting prey and hiding from predators.

Large eyes helped *Stenopterygius* see in dark, deep water.

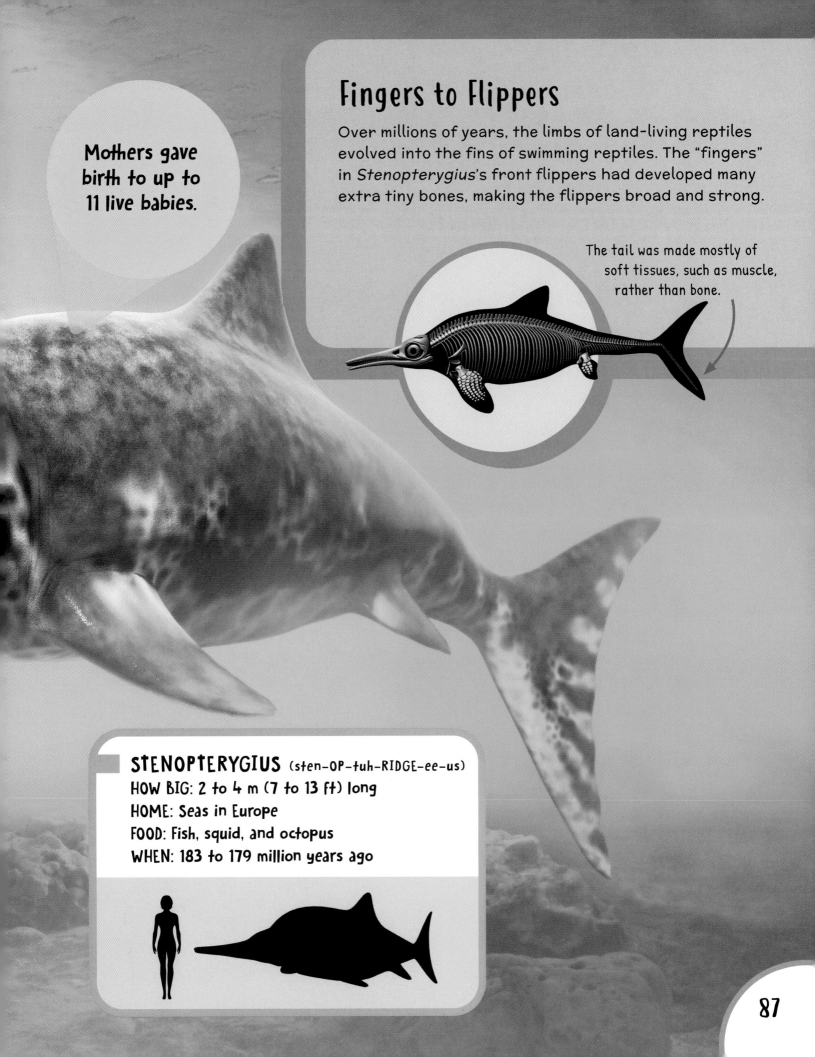

Mothers gave birth to up to 11 live babies.

Fingers to Flippers

Over millions of years, the limbs of land-living reptiles evolved into the fins of swimming reptiles. The "fingers" in *Stenopterygius*'s front flippers had developed many extra tiny bones, making the flippers broad and strong.

The tail was made mostly of soft tissues, such as muscle, rather than bone.

STENOPTERYGIUS (sten-OP-tuh-RIDGE-ee-us)
HOW BIG: 2 to 4 m (7 to 13 ft) long
HOME: Seas in Europe
FOOD: Fish, squid, and octopus
WHEN: 183 to 179 million years ago

SARCOSUCHUS

Sarcosuchus was a relative of today's crocodiles and alligators. Yet, at over 9 m (31 ft) long, it was much bigger than today's largest crocodile, the saltwater crocodile, which reaches 6 m (20 ft). Crocodile-like reptiles survived when an asteroid hit Earth 66 million years ago.

Sarcosuchus's skin was covered in hard, bony plates.

River Hunter

Sarcosuchus lived in and around rivers. Like today's crocodiles, it snapped up animals in the water, as well as crawling fast onto land to grab large animals looking for a drink.

Sarcosuchus could seize plant-eating dinosaurs as large as Ouranosaurus.

Like a Crocodile

Crocodile-like reptiles evolved at around the same time as dinosaurs. At first, they lived on land and were slim. Later, many grew bigger and, like today's crocodiles, had bony plates for protection.

Around 220 million years ago, *Hesperosuchus* was an early little crocodile-like reptile.

There were 132 sharp teeth in its long, strong jaws.

SARCOSUCHUS (SAR-ko-SOO-kus)
HOW BIG: 8 to 9 m (26 to 30 ft) long
HOME: Around rivers in Africa and South America
FOOD: Fish and dinosaurs
WHEN: 133 to 112 million years ago

MOSASAURUS

Mosasaurus was one of the largest swimming reptiles that ever lived, reaching 17 m (56 ft) long. With its big eyes, it could spot distant prey as it swam in the sunlit surface waters of the ocean. It could kill almost any animal it saw, by cutting and crushing with its huge jaws.

Losing Teeth

Mosasaurus teeth were constantly replaced. New teeth were always growing inside the roots of the old teeth. Human children grow their adult teeth in a similar way, with the new teeth pushing out the baby teeth.

These *Mosasaurus* teeth are sharp and cone-shaped, making them perfect for cutting through flesh.

It swam fast by waving its tail from side to side.

Disaster!

When an asteroid hit Earth 66 million years ago, the explosion made ocean water more acidic. This damaged the shells of little ocean animals—and killed them. The animals that fed on shellfish died, followed by the big animals that ate them, like *Mosasaurus*.

Mosasaurus ate smaller reptiles and fish, which in turn fed on shelled animals.

The jaws opened wide enough to swallow prey whole.

MOSASAURUS (MOH-sah-SORE-us)
HOW BIG: 7 to 17 m (23 to 56 ft) long
HOME: Atlantic Ocean
FOOD: Fish, octopus, birds, and reptiles
WHEN: 82 to 66 million years ago

ARCHELON

Archelon was a turtle, with a shell to protect its body. The biggest fossil of *Archelon* measures 4 m (13 ft) from flipper tip to flipper tip. When alive, this turtle weighed as much as a family car. Like today's sea turtles, *Archelon* crawled onto beaches to lay its eggs.

Leathery Shell

Archelon's shell was made of curving rib bones. Unlike the shells of most of today's turtles, the ribs were not covered by bony plates. Like the shell of today's leatherback turtle, the ribs were covered in tough, leathery skin.

Archelon's leathery shell was lighter than a bony shell.

Archelon was the biggest turtle that ever lived.

ARCHELON (AR-kee-lon)
HOW BIG: 3 to 4.5 m (10 to 15 ft) long
HOME: Inland seas in North America
FOOD: Shellfish, fish, and squid
WHEN: 80 to 74 million years ago

The hard, hooked beak was used for crushing shellfish.

Long Life

Like today's turtles, *Archelon* had a long life, reaching the age of 100 or more. Young turtles probably did not reach the safety of their full size until they were 20 or 30 years old.

Archelon had 10 "fingers" and 10 "toes," forming long flippers.

GLOSSARY

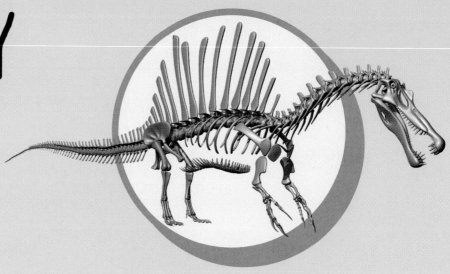

acidic
Able to wear away some materials.

amphibian
An animal that is born in water and breathes underwater using gills when young. As an adult, it usually breathes air using lungs and lives on land or in water. Today's amphibians include frogs and salamanders.

ankylosaur
A plant-eating dinosaur with a heavy body covered in plates, as well as a tail with a bony club at the end.

asteroid
A rocky object that orbits the Sun in space.

bird
An animal with a toothless beak, wings, and feathers. Females lay hard-shelled eggs on land. Birds evolved from meat-eating dinosaurs.

camouflage
The way the shade and shape of an animal make it less easy to see.

continent
A large area of land, usually separated from other continents by ocean. Today, there are seven continents: Africa, Antarctica, Asia, Australia, Europe, North America, and South America.

crest
A growth of bone, scales, feathers, skin, or hair on the head or back of an animal.

dinosaur
An extinct, land-living reptile that walked with its back legs held directly beneath its body.

extinct
When the last living member of an animal species has died.

evolve
To change over millions of years. An animal's body and habits may change slowly to suit the weather and landscape, or to better attack or escape from other animals.

feather
A light, fringed growth from the skin of birds and some dinosaurs. A feather has a tough central stem, with softer threads growing from either side. Feathers are made from keratin, also called horn, the same material that is found in scales and human hair.

flipper
A wide, flat, leg-like body part, used for swimming.

forest
A large area of land with many trees that are growing closely together.

fossil
The preserved remains of an animal or plant that lived in the distant past.

grassland
A wide area where most plants are grasses. Grasses did not become common until toward the end of dinosaur times.

hoof
Horn-covered toes.

horn
A tough, hard material, also called keratin, that is found in scales, feathers, beaks, claws, nails, and hair. Another meaning of "horn" is a pointed, bony growth on the head.

inland sea
A large area of water that lies within a continent.

limb
An arm, leg, or wing.

mammal
An animal that grows hair and feeds its babies on milk. Today's mammals include humans, whales, and cats.

migrate
To move from one area to another,
usually at the same time every year.

nodosaur
A plant-eating dinosaur with a heavy body
covered in bony plates.

oxygen
A gas that is in the air and is also part of
water. Animals need oxygen to live.

paleontologist (or palaeontologist)
A scientist who studies fossils.

plain
A large area of flat land.

plate
A bony, shield-like structure that grows
from deep within an animal's skin. The
skin that grows over a plate is often
covered by horn.

predator
An animal that hunts other animals.

prey
An animal that is killed by another
animal for food.

pterosaur
An extinct reptile with wings attached
to its extra-long fourth fingers.
A pterosaur was a relative
of dinosaurs.

relative
An animal that is a member
of the same group of similar
animals.

reptile
An animal that breathes air and usually
has scaly skin and lays eggs on land.

sauropod
A plant-eating dinosaur with a long
neck and a long tail.

scale
A small, hard plate that grows from the
top skin layer of most reptiles. Scales
are made from keratin, also called horn.
the same material as in feathers and
human hair.

shrub
A woody plant that is smaller than a tree
and usually has several stems.

species
A group of living things that look similar
and can make babies together.

spine
A long, pointed bone or body part.
Another meaning of "spine" is an
animal's backbone.

stegosaur
A plant-eating dinosaur with plates along
its back and pairs of spikes at the end of
its tail.

swamp
An area of low land where water collects,
making it wet and soft.

theropod
A meat-eating dinosaur that usually
walked on its two back legs, had hollow
bones and, usually, three main toes.

tissue
A body material, such as skin, fat,
or muscle.

woodland
Land with many trees and other plants.
The trees are far enough apart for
sunlight to reach the ground in places.

INDEX